# UNCONVENTIONAL LEADERSHIP

## BUILDING IMPACT

### 13 LESSONS FROM A GLOBAL EXECUTIVE IN THE DIGITAL AGE

**MARTIN E. GLASMACHER**

25+ Years – Executive, Coach, Author, Leader

DARE. LEAD. WIN. | emgex.ai

Hardcover ISBN: 979-8-9955083-2-8
Paperback ISBN: 979-8-9955083-1-1
E-book ISBN: 979-8-9955083-0-4

10   9   8   7   6   5   4   3   2   1

Printed in the United States of America

# Online Companion to Unconventional Leadership

For a free digital companion to this book, scan the QR code below. This will take you to a Self-Assessment Platform that's designed to help you measure, reflect on, and grow your leadership capabilities across the 13 dimensions explored in this book.

## How It Works

*Step 1: Take the Assessment*

- Rate yourself honestly on 65 statements drawn from the 13 chapters.

*Step 2: Receive Your Profile*

- Get your overall leadership profile: Developing, Emerging, Established, or Visionary.

*Step 3: Review Your Chapter Scores*

- See exactly where you are strongest and where the greatest growth opportunities lie, visualized across four charts.

*Step 4: Get AI Coaching:*

- Receive personalized, AI-generated coaching recommendations specific to your scores and each chapter topic.

*Step 5: Download Your Report*

- Save a fully formatted PDF report to review and share.

This platform exists for more than your development. A portion of ever
completed report contributes to the EMGEX Emerging Leaders Program–
funding stipends, coaching access, and educational resources for young leade:
around the world.

When you take this assessment, you are investing in yourself—and in the ne:
generation of global leaders.

Be one of them.

Access the free assessment at:
www.emgex.ai

# Table of Contents

# Introduction

From Germany's tech roots to U.S. boardrooms, European shop floors, Indian operations, R&D, critical business models, and global IT leadership, I've led many teams through transformation and uncertainty.

For 25 years, I've worked in many industries and different business environments and collaborated across cultures in many corners of the world. From launching my first software application product as an entrepreneur to learning how to design and build condominium complexes from the ground up, I've served as an executive, formed high-performing teams, and worked hands-on in operational environments. I've also stepped into coaching and joined an inter-company coaching leadership group. From project management to C-level leadership, each role has shaped how I learn and lead.

These experiences also taught me that leadership isn't universal—it's contextual. Understanding cultural nuances in different places around the world as well as in the office isn't a soft skill; it's a strategic advantage. The ability to adapt thoughtfully and connect authentically has shaped every success I've had.

The stories and lessons you're about to read are drawn from the many stages in my career—each one a window into the challenges, insights, and quiet victories that I believe define global leadership. They're about operating smart systems and processes that serve, creating teams that thrive, and building a legacy that endures.

Whether you're just starting out or leading at the highest level, I hope these reflections inspire you to think bigger, lead better, and live with purpose. Success isn't just about titles or milestones. It's about the impact you make and the lives you elevate along the way.

# How This Book Was Born

After decades of learned and earned leadership across several industries that included global challenges, a move to the United States from Germany, and being at the crux of the technical revolution in big businesses, I'm now at the stage of my career where I find myself reflecting on a journey that was shaped by moments I'll never forget. I decided recently it's time to document the milestones and the people behind them.

The idea took root: Turn these lifetime moments into a book. Not just for me, but to share with others the story of hard work, human connection, and fulfillment that comes from showing up, again and again.

I started with the present, and worked my way back through the years, gathering photos, resumés, letters of recommendation, and company announcements. I laid it all out and started writing. Before I knew it, I had a living archive of my career. I kept it close, revisiting it from time to time. Each time, I felt a deeper sense of gratitude and pride. The magnitude of what my colleagues and I had built together became clearer, and this book morphed into a reflection on what becomes possible when vision meets discipline and when leadership is grounded. It's an unconventional journey. At its core, this book is about people.

This book is for the builders, the dreamers, the quiet grinders who show up every day. It's for those who want to grow their careers, provide a good life for their families, and leave an impactful legacy. So read on. Reflect. Laugh a little. Most of all, believe in what's possible. If my story sparks something in you, it's already fulfilled its purpose.

*"A good book teaches. A great one resonates.*
*These reflections helped me aim for both."*

# Chapter 1:
# My Career, in Short

## The Early Years

My unconventional journey began in Birkesdorf, a small town near Cologne, Germany, where the hum of industry was everywhere. Machines roared, systems pulsed, and processes shaped daily life. If fascinated by how things worked, I was absolutely captivated by how they could be improved, scaled, and made resilient. These early years of my career weren't glamorous, but they were formative. They taught me that leadership is born in curiosity, forged in complexity, and strengthened by the people who walk beside you.

*"Cologne was the spark.*
*Scale became the story."*

In the late 1980s, I took on IT and project management roles that spanned automation controls, manufacturing, and enterprise systems at Voith, a global technology company. Voith built and serviced the biggest and fastest paper machines and was involved with the largest hydropower dams in the world. That scale taught me how to think in systems and processes.

At Voith, I led deployments of computer-aided engineering (CAE) and Enterprise Resource Planning (ERP) systems across Germany. I put together a tight-knit team of engineers, IT folks, analysts, and operators—each bringing precision and tenacity to the table.

Those early years shaped everything about my views on working hard and leading well. They taught me that leadership is more than authority. It's about clarity, collaboration, people, and the courage to drive change. My team and I learned to navigate complex situations together, to deliver with discipline, and to celebrate the wins, both big and small.

## From Concept ZERO to VPEX

The early 1990s were a time of restless possibility. Technology was shifting quickly, industries were searching flexibility, and entrepreneurs were stepping into the unknown with little more than determination. For me, those years were defined by testing ideas in real time and the thrill of building something that didn't exist before. This raw energy inspired me to form my own company.

Emgesoft was a software development company focused on building agile solutions for the insurance industry. At the time, most large insurers relied on rigid, centralized, mainframe architectures that struggled to support remote branches and local offices. We saw an opportunity to develop and deploy new software and database applications on Windows-based PC systems.

> *"Clarity is the compass,*
> *collaboration is the engine,*
> *and courage is the spark."*

I developed VPEX with a software engineer friend. This modular software suite was built on Superbase, a pioneer in Windows advanced database applications, for the emerging Microsoft Windows market. VPEX stood for *Verwalten, Planen, Expandieren*—Manage, Plan, Expand—and offered a comprehensive digital platform for client data, policy management, contract administration, sales team oversight, and reporting.

A few years later, my small team and I reached a major milestone when one of Germany's largest insurance companies invited us to present VPEX to their executive board, head of IT, and lead application development managers. I remember walking into the boardroom, connecting our system to their display, and demonstrating the future of decentralized insurance operations. That moment validated our vision and marked a turning point in our journey.

VPEX took us across Germany and into Italy, meeting clients face-to-face, customizing solutions, and helping businesses grow with tools perfectly suited to their needs. This was early leadership in action, full of questions, demands, and deep rewards. We built software, but we also built momentum for ourselves and trust.

Between 1994 and 2001, I cofounded and led multiple real estate ventures focused on high-end residential construction in my hometown in Germany. These projects combined entrepreneurial vision with disciplined execution, resulting in the successful development of several apartment buildings and multifamily homes.

Meanwhile, between 2000 and 2005, I served as a personal coach within Voith's internal leadership development initiative, supporting high-potential employees across multiple business units. This role was part of a strategic effort to cultivate future leaders and enhance cross-functional collaboration.

## The Leap

I've always been drawn to global travel and the idea of working abroad. I remember reading a story in a business magazine about someone who built a global career living and working across borders. I couldn't explain why at the time, but the idea captivated me: the chance to go abroad, meet new people, explore cultures, and discover new ways of thinking. So, my wife, daughter, and I did.

In 2005, we relocated to Raleigh, North Carolina, and I was tasked with
ding Voith's North American IT transformation, which included
vigating legacy platforms, global teams, and emerging technologies. Not
ly was I implementing systems and processes—I was shaping the digital
ckbone of a multinational business. In Raleigh, I began developing my
dership style: decisive, collaborative, and deeply strategic.

*"I've always believed in getting things done. Fix the problem,
empower the team, and move the business forward."*

## uilding the Foundation for Scale

Between 2005 and 2016, my role expanded, and I became CEO/CIO of
ith IT Solutions North America. I launched a global R&D (Research and
velopment) center for mobility tech. I also led major overhaul initiatives,
ile moving ERP support functions worldwide and rolling out global
siness applications for 25 manufacturing plants around the world. Beyond
grade, these were foundational shifts toward scalable, secure, future-ready
erations.

I worked directly with CEOs and boards, translating complex strategies
o business outcomes. Whether it was moving data centers off-premises or
fining IT strategy for billion-dollar businesses, I operated at the
ersection of vision and execution.

In the end, the story of my early years isn't about machines or systems,
t about possibility. From Birkesdorf to boardrooms across continents, I
rned that clarity is the compass, collaboration is the engine, and courage
he spark that carries you forward. Leadership is not reserved for the
osen few; it's built step by step, decision by decision. My hope is that as

you read on, you'll see that the lessons of these beginnings are not min
alone—they're tools for anyone ready to build, to grow, and to lead witl
purpose.

## Reflections on Growth

Careers aren't built overnight. They're shaped by choices, challenges, an
quite frankly, the simple determination to keep growing. My journey fror
Cologne to the C-suite was quiet and not at all flashy. I built my career as
leader with grit, humility, and a kind heart.

*"Success isn't reserved for the lucky few.*
*It's earned—step by step,*
*decision by decision, with grit, grace,*
*and a willingness to learn."*

## Questions to Consider

- What experiences have shaped the way you lead today?

- What kind of impact do you want your leadership to have on th
  people around you?

- If you were to document your own story, what themes, turnin
  points, or quiet victories would stand out?

- How do you want others to feel after working with you, and wh⟨
  choices can you make to reinforce that legacy?

# My Leadership Journey

**1988** — **IT Manager**
**Voith Paper**
Engineering, Manufacturing, Services
HQ Germany

**1990** — **Founder**
**emgesoft**
**Software development**
Software insurance industry
HQ Germany

**1995** — **Co-Founder**
**Real Estate Buildings**
Construction biz
Condominium complexes
HQ Germany

**2001** — **Coach**
**Voith Paper**
Workshop series TASK
Intercompany coaching
HQ Germany

**2005** — **CEO / CIO**
**Voith IT Solutions**
IT Backend Infrastructure, Application development, Security, Services
HQ USA

**2017** — **CIO**
**ARTERA Services**
Cloud Services, Application development, Security
HQ USA

**2018** — **Co-Chair**
**SIM – Society Information Management**
Premier network for IT leadership
HQ USA

**2026** — **CEO & Founder**
**EMGEX LLC**
Published Unconventional Leadership
Launched AI-powered EMGEX Leadership Assessment Platform
HQ USA

# Chapter 2:
# Startup Energy: Raw and Ready to Launch

When you start something from scratch, you become the engine at the heart of a forming ecosystem, driving vision, setting direction, shaping the roadmap, and holding the big picture together through round-the-clock effort. It's an exhilarating ride that gives you essential lessons and skills you'll need no matter where your career takes you.

I founded emgesoft in the 1990s to fill a sorely-needed gap. The startup provided a way to centralize information across decentralized teams. We sought to give our customers robust functionality with intuitive interfaces that would allow them to operate independently while staying aligned with their corporate systems. Simply speaking, we built early software that allowed branches of a corporation to communicate with its central office in real time. This was way before iPhones and even the Internet.

Back then, one of the biggest challenges for insurance companies in Germany was the lag in receiving month-end sales and team performance reports. Closing the books took days, delaying critical feedback to the branch managers and sales teams. Yet the business thrives on momentum. Strong sales and high-performing teams are its lifeblood. Leaders were urgently seeking ways to improve efficiency, streamline processes, and access real-time data.

That's where emgesoft's software, VPEX, stepped in. It not only filled the gap with better insights and reporting and faster data processing, but it also sparked conversations across branches. It became a catalyst for change among managers and team leaders alike.

As founder and head of product design, I led the development of the full software suite, authored user manuals, designed training curricula, and delivered hands-on workshops throughout Germany. We tailored implementations to each client and released frequent module updates to meet

ver-changing needs. It was a time of constant learning and adaptation, with
ew customers, challenges, and business models around every corner.



In the end, startups are more than companies—they're also classrooms.
very client meeting, late-night iteration, and boardroom pitch taught me
ssons that carried far beyond emgesoft. VPEX was proof that clarity can
merge from chaos and that momentum is built one bold move at a time.
he real gift of entrepreneurship is not the software you ship or the contracts
ou sign; it's a mindset of curiosity, resilience, and possibility that you earn
at keeps opening doors, wherever the journey leads next.

## Key Takeaways

- Startup energy can be raw and demanding, while also providing
  unforgettable lessons and experiences along the way. When you build
  something from nothing, you become the engine—the one who
  holds the vision, sets the pace, and keeps the momentum alive even
  when the path is unclear. Entrepreneurship teaches you quickly that
  clarity doesn't come from waiting. It comes from movement. From
  trying, adjusting, listening, and trying again.

- Your entrepreneurship years are a classroom. You learn to lead
  without a map, to stay close to the work, and to listen deeply to
  customers who often reveal the next opportunity before you see it
  yourself. You learn to empower teams and design systems that make
  their work visible and to prove that their input matters. You learn

that trust is built through presence—in workshops, in client meetings, in late-night brainstorms where the next breakthrough can be one conversation away.

- Entrepreneurship sharpens your instincts. It can teach you to adapt faster than the market, to stay hands-on even as responsibilities grow, and to lead with curiosity and quiet boldness. The real gift isn't the product you ship or service you provide—it is the mindset you earn. A mindset of resilience, possibility, and forward motion can shape every chapter of your leadership journey that follows.

## Questions to Consider

- Where in your current role could you bring more startup energy— speed, clarity, or hands-on leadership?

- What early-career lesson do you want to bring forward into your next chapter?

- How can you model now the same presence and engagement you valued during your entrepreneurial years?

# Chapter 3:
# From Prototype to Platform

Every transformation begins small with an idea sketched on paper, a prototype tested in the field, a team willing to try. My launchpad was PEX, where I learned how to start . . . and scale. Those early days taught me that innovation is about vision, courage, and persistence, as well as bringing people together, aligning them with purpose, and rallying them behind change. What began as hustle became momentum, and momentum became transformation.

*My* momentum led me to the boardroom. From building a system from scratch and leading my emgesoft team, I had learned how to drive transformation and to communicate change in a way that moved people. At this point in my career, my focus shifted, and this hustle became a blueprint for enterprise transformation and building and scaling systems that last.

## Strategic Transformation in Motion

By the early 2000s, transformation had become my calling card. My technical leadership in CAE and ERP systems evolved into a broader mission commanding IT infrastructure, application development, and global IT service delivery at Voith. Beyond manufacturing, Voith is a complex, multinational enterprise with billions in sales. I was privileged to help shape digital and mobile technology backbone.

As CEO and CIO of Voith IT Solutions North America, I led the charge to modernize legacy systems, migrate data centers, and implement cybersecurity frameworks that protected operations across the continent. We built cross-functional teams that aligned technology with business outcomes and made that alignment inevitable.

# Building the Mobility R&D Hub

One of our most transformative milestones at Voith was the launch of global R&D center dedicated to mobility technology. Far from a sid initiative, it was a bold strategic move that placed our business at the leadin edge of industrial innovation and digital transformation. It enabled mobile first solutions, seamless expert remote collaboration, and real-tim empowerment of sales teams and engineers at customer sites.

The idea was to integrate mobile devices and mobile applications int existing business processes, providing mobile access to folks on the road an engineers on the shop floor. (The beginning of using iPhones and iPads i the real business world!) This was a huge change because now you didn have to connect a laptop to a network or wait until you got to a hotel t connect to company business systems and data. This was the beginning o mobilizing the workforce, which is how we do business today.

We assembled an ambitious team that delivered real impact. They wer resourceful and ready for the challenge. The team quickly built stron connections with business units and engaged with strategic key technolog partners and suppliers. They explored emerging technologies, and crafted th initial vision and prototypes. From day one, we produced encouraging resul through steady, iterative progress.

This was about driving real transformation and leveraging mobil technology to boost efficiency, deliver and access real-time data at you fingertips, and unlock measurable ROI. Early innovations included mobi type camera-based diagnostics that streamed live images from plants, mill and shop floors back to headquarters. Our remote experts could localize an resolve issues in real time, which dramatically reduced downtime and trav costs. What once took days or weeks could now be solved in hours.

*"We brought the plant floor to the office—*
*and the experts to the problem. All in real time."*

## Safety, Efficiency, and Scale

Another breakthrough came in the realm of safety. Daily walkthroughs on the shop floor had long relied on paper forms, manual data entry, and time-consuming, back-office processing. We envisioned a smarter way: mobile apps on tablets that captured safety data instantly, with just a few taps.

The result?

- Real-time reporting

- Seamless data integration

- Global visibility across all plants

- Massive efficiency gains

- And most importantly, enhanced safety outcomes.

What began as a pilot in one plant quickly scaled across regions, and eventually, the globe. We didn't realize when our groundbreaking journey began that it would eventually be recognized at the highest level.

The team received an award from the world's largest independent, non-listed expert organization in the field of testing, inspection, and certification.

*Leadership Spotlight*

One leader on the team stood out. She never gave up—even when early results were disappointing and the vision looked uncertain. She seemed to get stronger when things got tough, keeping the team focused and moving. Her resilience became the driving force behind what ultimately became one of the first global mobile shopfloor safety systems in the industry, later recognized with a major award.

## Leading Change by Hitting the Road

Driving this kind of change wasn't easy. It meant convincing executives and plant managers, navigating language barriers, managing upfront costs, and rethinking IT infrastructure to support mobile integration. I knew that transformation required more than vision—it required allies.

So I hit the road. We built trust, gathered support, and started small. One plant. One team. One prototype. Then we iterated, learned, failed, refined— and scaled . . . fast.

> *"Start with a sketch. Build a team.*
> *Learn fast. Scale faster."*

Scaling is about vision carried forward. A prototype proves what's possible, but scaling turns possibility into progress. Each pilot, each iteration, each alliance built across borders became part of a larger rhythm: transformation that lasts. Mobility technology redefined what we believed was achievable. And those lessons endure. Begin with courage, build with clarity, and keep moving. When leaders choose to scale with purpose, they don't just deliver innovation—they shape the future.

## Key Takeaways

- Every transformation begins small. A prototype, spark, or first version proves what's possible. Turning that spark into a platform requires discipline, clarity, and alignment. Technology only creates impact when it's tied directly to business outcomes. Strategy must drive every system, every architecture, every line of code.

- Scaling from prototype to platform also demands trust. Change doesn't travel on process charts; it travels on relationships. When teams feel connected, informed, and included, they adopt faster, collaborate better, and build with more confidence. Empowering people with the right tools—particularly mobility technology—is about more than mere convenience. It's about capability. It's about giving teams the power to act, decide, and deliver wherever they are.

- At the center of all of it is safety. Innovation thrives when people feel safe—physically, emotionally, and operationally. When leaders protect their teams, performance follows. Safety creates the conditions for experimentation, iteration, and bold thinking.

- Scaling a prototype into a platform is a leadership journey built on clarity, trust, empowerment, and the courage to build systems that serve people—not the other way around.

## Questions to Consider

- How can you empower your teams with tools that increase capability, not just convenience?

- What steps can you take to ensure physical, operational, and psychological safety become foundations for innovation?

- Where might your next platform already be hiding inside a simple prototype?

# Chapter 4:
# Global Perspective

I began my career in the structured, precision-driven world of German engineering and manufacturing. In 2005, I made the bold move of relocating to Raleigh, North Carolina, to lead Voith's North American IT transformation. This decision demanded new ways of thinking.

At first, the contrast felt daunting. I now had two worlds, two cultures, two sets of expectations. There are different ways of approaching things, different vibes in the office, different methods of engagement. Over time, I came to see one big gift. Leadership isn't about choosing one culture over the other; it's about blending structure with speed, discipline with adaptability, and shaping a vision that transcends borders.

This cultural shift isn't just geographical—it's philosophical. I had to learn how to navigate different business cultures, leadership and communication styles, and organizational dynamics. Over time, I learned to combine German rigor with American agility. I blended discipline with adaptability.

*"Germany taught me structure.*
*The U.S. taught me speed.*
*Together, they shaped how I lead."*

## Preparing for the Leap

Before my family and I made the move to the U.S., I spent time reflecting on the cultural differences between Germany and America—especially how they might show up in everyday business interactions. At home, we all heard

e stories: Americans like small talk, they're optimistic, and their rhythms of
mmunicate differ from ours. But I didn't want to rely on hearsay. I wanted
understand the dynamics and nuances of American business culture.

I hired an American personal coach who had corporate experience and
ecialized in developing human potential to help me tackle this segue. We
orked one-on-one, almost daily, for several weeks. We explored everything:
ne, timing, expectations . . . even how to begin a phone conversation.

I clearly remember one of my first assignments. I had to call one of our
R managers in the U.S. to discuss staffing. In Germany, that would've been
direct, no-frills conversation. Efficient, to the point, and done. But my
ach walked me through what to expect, and he nailed it. From the very
st minute, the call felt warm, familiar, almost like we'd known each other
r years. The small talk, the pacing, and the tone all unfolded exactly as
edicted and not at all like anything I was used to.

That experience taught me that cultural fluency is a strategic asset. That
l was just one of many moments where preparation paid off. Investing in
at coaching gave me the confidence to lead with empathy, adapt with
ention, and build trust from day one.

## arewell, Birkesdorf

Before we packed up and moved to the States, we said farewell to family
d lifelong friends. What a celebration it was. During one of our final
enings in town, we threw a goodbye party that filled every corner of our
me with laughter, music, and memory. A *bierwagen* (like a food truck for
er) rolled into the front yard. Barbecue grills fired up in the back. And
n, like a scene from a storybook, the marching band *Tambourcorps Einigkeit
kesdorf* arrived, playing the soundtrack of our small-town life. My wife and
hook more than 200 hands and shared countless hugs. We said goodbye
only way we knew how: shoulder to shoulder, heart to heart. Leaving
sn't easy.

*"That night reminded us what  
we were carrying with us."*

Everybody knows you never forget home. Family and friends hold a place that time and distance can't erase. Crossing an ocean meant leaving a lot behind, but it never broke the bonds. Every visit back to Germany is a reminder of how strong those connections remain. We go back regularly, and it's always worth it. Traditional festivals in the town where we grew up, meaningful family celebrations, and reunions with friends who've been part of the journey from the beginning. The laughter, the stories, the sense of belonging. It's a blast every time.

## What I Took With Me

Often the smallest things carry the greatest weight.

While packing up and sorting through our things before moving, I paused and stared at what I held in my hands. It was the seasonal Orden, a Carnival medal given to all active members of our hometown Karnevalsclub, a German association dedicated to organizing carnival festivities and traditions (where I'm still a proud member). It was created for the millennium year and displays the club motto for the 2000 season. The medal shows two landmarks: our beloved St. Peter's Church in Birkesdorf and the iconic Empire State Building in New York.

The tagline reads: "In BIRKESDORF and USA, the year 2000 is now here."

What a surprise. I was flooded with joy. I took it with me to the States and placed it in my office. It hangs to this day.

Every time I see the medal, I'm reminded of where I come from. Of family. Of friends. Of growing up in a small town in Germany where laughter echoed through the streets and traditions stitched us together.

It's just a medal, but it's also a bridge between past and present, between continents, between who I was and who I've become.

## Living the Cross-Border Life

Navigating boardrooms in North Carolina and factory floors in Berlin and scaling startups in Mumbai while working with teams in São Paulo shaped a worldview few get to earn.

Each project and region added a new lens. The rhythm of local traditions, the nuance of language, the shared laughter over late-night strategy sessions. This journey broadened my horizons and forged a leadership style rooted in empathy. Wherever the challenge, I move with purpose. People first. Always forward. It's truly the people and cultures that bind it all together. That's the clue. That's the gift.

*"Leadership without borders.*
*Humanity at the center."*

## Culture Eats Strategy—We Learned That the Hard Way

We've all heard the phrase *culture eats strategy for breakfast*. For us, it wasn't just a saying—it was reality.

Understanding global team dynamics and cultural nuance isn't a nice-to-have. It's mission-critical. To help our U.S.-based management team better navigate cross-border collaboration, we hosted an intercultural management workshop focused on German business culture. We brought in a German coach and spent two full days diving into the key differences in communication styles, decision-making rhythms, and the subtle signals that shape trust. It was eye-opening.

Suddenly, our team in North Carolina understood why emails from abroad felt "too direct." They learned how to approach global meetings with more cultural sensitivity, and what it meant to truly collaborate across the ocean. That workshop transformed how we worked together by building empathy, sharpening awareness, and laying the foundation for deeper trust across our global teams.

Strategy sets the direction. Culture determines whether you get there together.

## Travel Isn't Just Movement—It's Momentum.

I'm grateful for the global connections and friendships forged while working in the U.S. Each region brings its own rhythm, its own drivers, and its own wisdom. Immersing yourself in different cultures and approaches broadens perspectives and sharpens leadership. You learn what resonates, what motivates, and how to avoid costly missteps when crafting and

ommunicating new visions and directions. In a world of global initiatives
hat draw people from far-reaching places, proximity matters.

In other words, being there in person builds trust, accelerates alignment,
nd turns strategy into shared reality.

Today, I live in Charleston, South Carolina, with my wife Uschi, and we
maintain deep ties to both the U.S. and Germany. Our daughter, Lea, a
raduate of UNCW with a master's in education and ESL, now lives in
harleston with her husband Jackson. It feels like our family's journey has
ome full circle.

Home isn't one place but a network of people, values, and experiences
hat shape you.

## Leading Across Cultures

Whether managing global business applications rollout or mentoring a
ross-functional team, I adapt my approach to fit the context while not
ompromising on outcomes.

I'm fluent in the language of transformation, whether speaking to
ngineers in Cologne or executives in New York. My leadership is global not
ust in scope, but in spirit. True leadership transcends borders. It connects
eople, aligns purpose, and builds bridges between ideas and execution.

> *"When you lead with respect and clarity,*
> *geography becomes a strength—not a barrier."*

In the end, global leadership is defined by genuine understanding and
mpathy. Strategy may set the direction, but culture determines whether you
rive together. My experiences taught me that leadership without borders
eans humanity at the center: listening deeply, respecting differences, and
uilding bridges that turn diversity into strength. Home is the network of

people, values, and experiences that shape you. When leaders embrace that truth, they don't just lead across cultures; they lead across generations.

## Key Takeaways

- Good global leadership begins with empathy and understanding. When you lead across borders, culture becomes context instead of constraint. It shapes how people communicate, make decisions, build trust, and interpret strategy. Great leaders don't ignore those differences; they honor them. They translate global vision into something locally actionable, meaningful, and real.

- Working across continents teaches you to stay anchored. Family, values, and personal principles become the constants that keep you grounded when everything around you shifts. Adaptation becomes a daily practice. You learn to flex your style without compromising your standards and adjust your approach without losing your center.

- At the heart of global leadership is connection. True leadership builds bridges between regions, functions, and people who may never sit in the same room but share the same mission. When leaders connect people, not just processes, teams move with more trust, clarity, and unity.

- A global perspective isn't something you acquire just from travel. It's earned through the willingness to see the world through someone else's eyes. It's the quiet confidence that comes from knowing that leadership doesn't scale unless empathy does too.

uestions to Consider

- What do you think are some consequences of leading globally without your team understanding the different cultures that are part of the strategy?

- Where do you need to translate a global vision into something more locally actionable?

- Which personal anchors (values, relationships, routines) keep you grounded when leading across borders?

- Who are the people, teams, or regions you need to build stronger bridges with?

# Chapter 5:
# Leadership Is a Call to Action

As I boarded the plane to Mumbai in 2008, to address a major issue with a consulting firm, I carried more questions than certainty. We needed to close a critical gap in one of our global system support models, and wasn't sure if the effort would succeed. The stakes were enormous. The global systems ran 24/7, customers depended on us in every time zone, and a team back home was skeptical that trust could travel across oceans. If we failed, the cost would be more than financial. It would be sleepless nights, frustrated team members and users, and a blow to the very confidence that keeps teams moving forward.

The thing is that leadership isn't about waiting for certainty. It's about stepping into doubt and showing up anyway. That's why I boarded that plane. Not just to negotiate contracts or review processes, but to look people in the eye and say, "You are part of this team."

## When Scale Demands Boldness

Big problems demand bold decisions, and in this case, I made one of the most transformative calls of our leadership journey.

Supporting global enterprise resource planning (ERP) systems with 24/7 availability meant maintaining nonstop operations for customers around the world. That required round-the-clock technical system support—three shifts a day, every day of the year. The cost was staggering. Beyond our primary teams, we needed backup crews and third-level experts on standby. Operating under this existing model was becoming unsustainable.

We needed a new approach that balanced reliability with cost efficiency. That's when we explored something partnering with a consulting and third-level technical support firm based in Mumbai, India.

The idea sparked immediate skepticism within our team. Trust was the central concern. Could remote support feel local? Could offshore colleagues truly integrate into our rhythm?

## *Leadership Spotlight*

One of our finance managers was the steady partner every executive needs. He always had a clear view of the company's financial health—cutting waste while keeping the big picture in mind. In discussions about major initiatives, he consistently delivered the right financial insight at the right moment. His grounded perspective helped shift the narrative and guide smarter decisions.

## Leading by Example

I knew this initiative needed leadership by example. So I boarded that plane to Mumbai and sat down with the team face-to-face. My goal was clear: I needed to make them feel like they were sitting right next door to our U.S. office.

We aligned on processes, streamlined communication, and embedded them into our daily routines with online meetings, instant messaging tools, shared dashboards. No barriers. No silos.

The result was groundbreaking. We achieved seamless 24/7 system support for global operations at a fraction of the original cost. More importantly, we built a support network that felt local and connected, not just by technology, but by trust, rhythm, and shared purpose. Over three intense months, we trained relentlessly, hosted onsite visits with key players, and prepared to launch a remote support model for the backend infrastructure of a global ERP system that served hundreds of users across 25 manufacturing sites in every time zone on the planet.

We didn't stop there. We added another highly technical backend process to the task list for our new remote team: the weekly deployment of custom-built software packages to the production system. It was a demanding task, requiring expert skills and carrying significant responsibility. It became another major success, with our U.S.-based team no longer required to work night shifts.

This milestone was about more than operational efficiency. It was about redefining what global teamwork could look like and proving that with the right mindset, distance disappears.

> *"When remote teams feel local, magic happens.*
> *Communication becomes rhythm.*
> *Collaboration becomes instinct."*

A shift of this magnitude doesn't happen overnight. In this case, it demanded exceptional fundamentals to succeed, not just for our service technician teams, but for the hundreds of internal users who depended on a single global business system, operating round-the-clock. The real groundwork meant going deep under the hood. Documentation was a cornerstone, and technical processes and system protocols had to be crystal clear and up to par.

Paper alone wasn't enough. We also flew key members of our remote support team from Mumbai to the U.S., hosting intensive sessions focused on support, process alignment, and system understanding. Yes, knowledge transfer was an important reason for this, but it was also about connection. I wanted them to meet our people, understand our culture, and build trust with our technical leads.

Only after we felt every box was checked, all processes aligned, all relationships built, and all goals met, did we make the move. From that point on, our teams in Mumbai became an integral part of supporting a truly global system.

Leadership is never just about goals. True leadership is about people, trust, and the courage to act when the path is uncertain. What began as a logistical challenge became proof that distance is only a barrier if we allow it to be. When leaders choose presence and listen across boundaries and build bridges instead of walls, they discover that global teamwork is a catalyst and not a compromise. The lesson is simple but enduring: When trust travels, leadership becomes unstoppable.

## Key Takeaways

- Leadership across distance demands presence. When teams are spread across time zones and cultures, people don't just need information; they need to feel that their leader is *with* them, even when they're thousands of miles away. Showing up with presence becomes the anchor that steadies a team navigating uncertainty. Your tone, your timing, and your attention matter.

- Trust grows when leaders listen deeply, especially when the hours don't line up neatly. Listening across time zones is an act of respect that tells people their voice matters, their context matters, and their challenges are seen. When skepticism inevitably surfaces, as it does in every global team, sincerity is the bridge. Saying, "You're part of this team," only works when your actions prove it.

- Distance doesn't have to dilute belonging. Great leaders make remote feel local by creating rhythms of communication that bring people together, no matter where they sit. Consistency becomes a source of clarity. Collaboration becomes instinct. Over time, the world feels smaller—not because technology connects us—but because trust transforms us.

- Making big calls is never just about the decision itself; it's about the leadership behind it. Bold decisions require leaders to be visible, especially when the stakes are high and uncertainty is thick. People look for steadiness, for someone willing to step forward and own the moment. When you show up fully, intentionally, and without hesitation, you signal the team isn't facing the unknown alone.

- Trust becomes the currency that carries those decisions across borders. It doesn't travel through systems or dashboards; it travels through people. Through conversations. Through consistency. Through the sense that even from thousands of miles away, your team knows you're in it with them. Presence is about emotional proximity. It's the feeling that your leader is close, even when geography says otherwise.

- Embedding remote teams into the rhythm of the business is part of that presence. When people feel included in the cadence and not just the process, they stop feeling like an extension and start feeling like an essential part of the whole. That's when global teamwork becomes something more than coordination. It becomes alignment. It becomes purpose. When purpose aligns, distance disappears.

- In the end, leading through distance and doubt, and making the big calls that come with it, is less about authority and more about connection. Leaders who show up, build trust, and create belonging across borders make decisions, but more importantly, they move people. And when people move together, even the biggest calls become shared victories.

## Questions to Consider

- When your team is spread across time zones, what does "showing up" look like beyond simply being available online?

- In moments of uncertainty, how do you make your presence felt in a way that builds trust rather than pressure?

- What rhythms of communication help your remote teams feel embedded in the business?

- When you make a big call, how do you ensure the decision (and the purpose behind it) travels clearly across borders?

# Chapter 6:
# Leading from the Center

I'll never forget the moment the system began to strain. What had started as a flawless cutover quickly unraveled as Europe came online. The room filled with tension, and in that instant, I felt the weight of every plant, transaction, and colleague depending on us. Doubt crept in. Had we missed something? Could the system hold?

Crisis doesn't wait for certainty. It demands presence. In that moment, leadership meant stepping into the center, not standing on the sidelines.

## Crisis Calls for Centered Leadership

One major critical situation we faced at Voith was a key global system performance issue during a new IT system rollout that forced me to move into crisis mode.

Our IT engineering and consulting teams had spent months preparing for a major technical upgrade to our global ERP system—one of the core business applications supporting hundreds of users across dozens of manufacturing plants worldwide. This was a mission-critical global platform. It had to work everywhere, every time.

Due to technical system support requirements from one of our key vendors, we had to replace the entire application and database backend environment. After extensive testing and scenario planning, we made the call to cut over from the old platform to the new one.

The project management office team was a critical part of my delivery organization. It orchestrated every phase: cutover plans, final readiness checks, and go-live decision calls with stakeholders. Green lights were given. Final testing passed. User accounts were remapped. The system went live.

The first wave of users in China logged on during their morning hours. Everything ran smoothly. High fives around the table. However, as Europe came online, the system began to strain. More users entered, performance dipped, and support calls surged.

I moved the cutover project and the entire team into crisis mode. The boardroom became a war room. Leaders from every project stream gathered. This moment demanded leadership from the center—visible, decisive, and fully engaged.

This system was front-and-center for all plants, departments, and management teams. Stakeholders demanded updates. It was crucial to provide clear, frequent guidance on the situation. Communication was key.

In a crisis, keeping people informed builds trust and alignment. Leadership means owning the narrative, not just the fix. When people understand what's happening, they rally. They support. They stay on board.

We quickly discovered the issue was tied to system load. A threshold of active user loads triggered a performance collapse, despite months of design sessions with engineers from Oracle, Microsoft, and other partners.

Finger-pointing wasn't an option. I brought everyone in. The next morning, our core technology partners arrived, and stayed. To give you a sense of the scale and intensity of the crisis we managed, we kept the crisis team together for five straight days. Day and night, experts controlled the situation from the nerve center. Three major global technology companies had team members physically present. After intense sessions, we uncovered the root cause: a memory compatibility issue between core database components and the server's Windows operating system. The problem only surfaced under specific load conditions. This explained why China's first shift ran smoothly.

*"Leadership isn't about titles—it's about presence.*
*In crisis, clarity is your currency."*

When systems fail, people look for clarity. In that moment, real leadership becomes presence. It's about turning a boardroom into a command center, and turning partners into teammates. We didn't solve the problem by escalation, but instead, by collaboration. By camping out, shoulder to shoulder, until the issue was fixed. That's what leading from the center looks like.

## Leadership Spotlight

When things became truly challenging and system issues were impacting people around the globe, one manager stepped up in a way I'll never forget. He worked around the clock on calls, in team chats, holding everything together with sheer commitment. His focus and endurance kept the operation moving when it mattered most.

## Zero Transactions Lost

Within 48 hours, we released a temporary fix—a newly defined system algorithm for memory balancing. While we still needed to monitor and frequently adjust certain system parameters, the algorithm stabilized the environment, controlled user load, and ensured uninterrupted business continuity around the clock.

Following the system failure and the countless discussions and discoveries in that ops center, Microsoft announced a global change to its technical support agreement for this class of Windows operating systems, all within 48 hours. Without that shared commitment of being in the room together, we wouldn't have made it.

We then designed and deployed a twin-system environment for our global manufacturing operations, integrating Microsoft's new system and support updates for testing within 72 hours.

The good news is that we never lost the system, or even a single business transaction. Even more, the experience deepened our partnerships—elevating collaboration to new heights.

*"Systems can fail, but trust cannot."*

In the end, the crisis wasn't defined by the glitch, but instead, by how we came together and faced it head-on. Five days in the war room proved that leadership in crisis is not about titles or escalation, but presence, partnership, and clarity. Systems can fail, but trust cannot. When leaders own the message, stay in the zone, and turn partners into teammates, they transform chaos into collaboration. That's what leading from the center means: Be the calm in the storm, the voice in the noise, and the presence that keeps the world turning when everything else feels uncertain.

## Key Takeaways

- In moments of crisis, silence is never neutral—it creates uncertainty, fuels assumptions, and leaves teams to fill the gaps with their own fears. Leadership in these moments begins with communication. Not polished speeches or perfect answers, but presence. When people don't know what's happening, they look to the center, the person willing to step forward and speak with clarity.

- Being front and center is about responsibility, not ego. Visibility builds confidence. When leaders show up consistently, calmly, and with purpose, teams feel anchored. They know who is guiding the ship and watching the horizon. And they know they're not navigating the storm alone.

- Clarity becomes the lifeline. People need updates, direction, and a sense of what comes next. They need to understand not only the facts, but the intentions behind decisions. Honest, frequent communication earns credibility, especially when the news is difficult. Trust grows when leaders tell the truth, especially when the truth is uncomfortable.

- Leading from the center also means leading the narrative. If you don't shape the message, someone else will. Clear communication aligns teams, invites support, and turns confusion into coordinated action. In the toughest moments, leadership becomes a partnership. Solutions emerge not from escalation, but from collaboration—staying in the room, shoulder to shoulder, until the path forward becomes clear.

- In the fog of crisis, communication is your compass. It steadies the team, sharpens focus, and reminds everyone that leadership isn't about having all the answers. It's about showing up, speaking clearly, and guiding people through uncertainty with honesty and resolve.

## Questions to Consider

- When a crisis hits, how quickly do you step forward to own the message. What would stepping forward sooner look like?

- Which team or stakeholder group needs more visibility from you right now, and what is one action you can take this week to show up for them?

- How can you create a communication rhythm that reduces uncertainty before it has a chance to grow?

- In your next high-pressure situation, what will you do to stay in the room and lead through partnership rather than escalation?

# Chapter 7:
# The Digital Shift: Leading Tech in PE-Centric Firms

The first thing I noticed when stepping into a private equity-owned business was the pace. Decisions were urgent . . . and relentless. Every meeting carried the weight of ROI, every initiative was measured against exit readiness, and every leader was expected to deliver under pressure. I had led transformations before, but this felt different. Here, speed was the language and results were the currency. I knew my technology background and years of global leadership had prepared me, but I also knew I was entering a world where transformation wasn't optional. It was the job.

Until 2017, I had navigated both entrepreneurial ventures and corporate leadership. Stepping into a new industry and a business owned by private equity was a leap into a new arena of ownership, accountability, and high-stakes leadership. At this point, it was a perfect opportunity to apply what had previously learned from German engineering and the unique leadership skills I had developed over many years. The challenges were real, and the culture was different. Change was the job.

What I discovered was that transformation at scale demands more than expertise—it demands vision, velocity, strong focus on ROI, and the ability to communicate change from the ground floor to the boardroom.

## From Strategy to Systems

By the time I joined the U.S. energy business, Artera, in 2017, the company was already a formidable force in both energy and construction. But its digital backbone—and its strategic potential—were still evolving.

As CIO and a member of the executive leadership team, I not only stepped in to lead the IT organization. I also created the vision and strategy, and then led the execution of new systems and processes to support explosive growth while building a team capable of sustaining it.

In just four years, we transformed from a multi-hundred-million-dollar business into a multi-billion-dollar enterprise. We expanded across 80+ locations and deployed over 25,000 pieces of fleet and equipment. My role was to align technology with operational excellence and strategic growth ambition and to build the infrastructure that could carry us forward.

> *"Growth at that scale isn't just about adding headcount or assets—it's about building systems that can absorb complexity and deliver clarity."*

## Building the Digital Core

My team and I led a sweeping modernization of the IT infrastructure. We migrated data centers off-prem, implemented cloud services, and rolled out ERP systems and new business applications across multiple operating companies. Our cybersecurity strategy incorporated robust Risk Governance and Cyber Risk Management, strengthened Identity and Zero-Trust controls, and advanced threat-detection measures. Our work ensured resilience across a sprawling, high-risk environment.

We also quickly recognized untapped potential and introduced field service tools, automated invoicing, and digital sales systems that empowered frontline teams with sharper focus and greater efficiency. These weren't just tech upgrades; they were operational accelerators.

Working in a business backed by large private equity firms fundamentally shifts your operating lens—especially around execution, delivery strengths, EBITDA, and shareholder relationships. Boards are hands-on, and leadership is expected to deliver clarity, agility, and results. For IT leaders, this means more than just keeping systems running. It's about enabling rapid pivots, supporting scalable growth, and being exit-ready at all times.

Every initiative must align with the business's investment thesis. Cost discipline is financial and cultural. Projects must be planned with precision and finished with urgency. In this environment, leadership means navigating complexity while staying focused on value creation. IT leadership, in particular, becomes a driver of transformation, not just a support function.

Shifting core system elements to the cloud was a strategic leap. Suddenly, we had a playground for innovation: a dynamic environment where ideas could be tested, tweaked, and launched at lightning speed. We built a system that let us experiment fast, fail smart, learn quickly, and deploy in bite-sized bursts, and then do it all over again. That rhythm became our edge. In the high-stakes world of private equity, agility is oxygen. Transformation is never easy, but with the right partners amplifying our strengths, not only did we keep pace, but we also led. The results were game-changing.

We had one manager on the team who was a true finance leader whose insight into the business always stood out. While others were still discussing problems and possible fixes, he was already implementing the solution. He didn't care about the spotlight; he cared about progress. Quiet, fast, and effective, he tackled issues before most people finished describing them.

## Leading Through Complexity

Our business spanned gas distribution, power delivery, municipal services, and specialty construction. Leading IT in this environment required technical fluency and strategic foresight. We negotiated MSEA license agreements, drove IT cost reductions, and changed the cybersecurity footprint to ensure compliance and scalability.

But the real and lasting transformation came from people. We built a culture of global teamwork, integrating systems and talent across geographies. My leadership extended into talent development, operational strategy, and executive alignment. I've always believed that transformation isn't just about systems and processes. Transformation is about people, trust, and shared ownership.

*"Technology is the engine—*
*but people are the fuel.*
*When you align both, you build*
*something unstoppable."*

The digital shift was never just about keeping pace with private equity expectations. It was about proving that technology could be the lever for transformation. People are the force that made it possible. Systems gave us scale, but trust gave us speed. In an environment where urgency is constant and results are measured in months and quarters, leadership means turning pressure into progress. When vision aligns with velocity, and technology aligns with talent, growth stops being a target and becomes a trajectory. That's the power of leading the digital shift: building not just for today's demands, but for tomorrow's possibilities.

## Key Takeaways

- Leading technology inside a private-equity environment demands a different kind of leadership—one shaped by speed, scrutiny, and relentless pressure to deliver measurable results. In PE-backed firms, priorities shift quickly, decisions accelerate, and leaders must translate complexity into clarity faster than ever. Leadership isn't just about modernizing systems; it's about modernizing mindsets.

- In these environments, technology becomes a strategic lever. Leaders must align IT with business outcomes as a driver of value creation. That means making tough calls, simplifying what's overly complex, and building systems that scale faster than the business itself. When systems grow ahead of the curve, they create stability in the middle of motion and give teams the confidence to move quickly without losing control.

- Cybersecurity becomes foundational for energy businesses where the stakes are high, the pace is unforgiving, and resilience is a strategic advantage. Protecting the business isn't just an IT responsibility; it's a leadership responsibility. The leaders who treat cybersecurity as a core part of value creation instead of a cost center set their organizations up for long-term strength.

- Empowering the field—the plants, the crews, the technicians, the sales teams—is where transformation becomes real. When frontline teams have tools that remove friction and deliver real-time insight, they don't just adopt technology; they accelerate it. Transformation doesn't start in the boardroom. It starts on the ground.

- None of this matters without alignment. Strategy is only as strong as the systems that support it. Leaders must connect vision with execution, ensuring that every initiative, every investment, and every roadmap ties back to measurable business outcomes. When people understand the "why," they commit to the "how."

- Ultimately, people drive progress. Technology enables it, but trust sustains it. In PE-backed environments, pressure is constant and expectations are high. Leaders must create clarity, offer direction, and build confidence. When they do, teams thrive. And when leaders combine courage, clarity, and connection, they turn pressure into progress and transformation into momentum.

## Questions to Consider

- What is one legacy system or process you can simplify or modernize to help your organization move faster?

- Where can you empower frontline teams with tools or insights that would immediately improve decision-making or efficiency?

- What step can you take this month to better align your IT roadmap with measurable business outcomes?

- How can you create more stability and clarity for your team during periods of rapid change or PE-driven pressure?

# Chapter 8:
# From White Space to Impact

During my years at emgesoft in the 1990s, our goal was to empower decentralized teams with robust functionality and intuitive interfaces, enabling them to operate independently while staying aligned with corporate systems. These were early days when it came to technology: no internet, no smart phones, no social media.

One of the biggest challenges was the lag in receiving month-end sales and team performance reports. Closing the books took days, delaying critical feedback to the branch managers and sales teams, and leaders were urgently seeking ways to improve efficiency, streamline processes, and access real time data.

As founder and head of product design at emgesoft, I started with a blank sheet of paper. I drew boxes that signified problems we were attempting to solve.

From these visualizations, we were able to tailor implementation of our modular software suite (VPEX [see page 9]). VPEX filled the gaps, and also more importantly, sparked conversations across branches, becoming a catalyst for change among managers and team leaders alike.

Every transformation I've led has started the same way—with an empty sheet. At first glance, any blank space can feel daunting, silent, unformed . . . waiting. But I've learned over the years that emptiness is simply possibility. The moment you sketch the first line, or write the first words, the vision begins to live. This alone can create momentum for the whole team in the hands of a good leader. That's the power of the white space. It invites leaders to imagine boldly, share openly, and build futures that others can see and believe in.

*"The empty sheet is where leadership begins.*
*It's where vision becomes visible."*

## From Blank Space to Shared Future

One of the most powerful realizations when starting from scratch—whether solving a problem, designing a new solution, or building part of an organization—is that you can't shape something you can't see. I have been in endless meetings talking about stuff for hours (sometimes weeks), only to find out that we still didn't clearly understand each other. Talking and visualizing even in the simplest way, can help change the misunderstanding. Putting ideas on paper can bring clarity. It turns abstract, perhaps jumbled, thoughts into something you can share, refine, and rally others around. Visibility kick-starts momentum. The moment it's sketched, it starts to live. This is how I developed and communicated clear and group-owned visions.

That blank space—whether it's a whiteboard, a flip chart, or a digital canvas—is alive with possibility. It's the starting point for every idea, every strategy, every transformation. While staring at that blank sheet can feel daunting, it's also exhilarating, because it means you're about to create something that didn't exist before.

Invite others to contribute. You'll be amazed how quickly clarity spreads. There's a unique satisfaction in watching your first sketches evolve. Concepts take shape, ideas connect, and suddenly, what was once abstract becomes real. It's like building a mosaic or solving a puzzle. Piece by piece, the big picture emerges, and when it does, it's deeply rewarding for everyone involved. Visualization suddenly becomes vision.

## Visualize to Energize

In Voith's coaching and workshop series TASK (a specialized program focused on team orientation and synergy, work and process methodology, communication, and collaboration), visualization was a cornerstone. Too often, we assume we're aligned in meetings only to discover later that we were talking past each other. A simple sketch, a diagram, or a shared canvas can change the entire dynamic.

During one TASK session, we had been discussing a cybersecurity model for hours. It was a good discussion, with lots of smart ideas and plenty of opinions. But the breakthrough didn't happen until someone grabbed a marker and started sketching the model together.

We laid out the core components in a few simple boxes. Then we connected the workstreams, added rough budget ranges underneath, and estimated timelines for each area. Within minutes, we had something we hadn't achieved through conversation alone: a shared picture of the whole effort on a single page.

For the first time, everyone in the room felt aligned. You could see the shift—clarity, confidence, and a sense of "we've got this." That one page became the anchor. Teams used it repeatedly in their own meetings, referring back to the page as the starting point for planning and execution.

This exercise helped us see the same future at the same time, and that alignment is what got the project moving.

## Leading Through Visualization

What I've found time and again is that teams appreciate the leader who starts and is willing to take the first step, even if the lines aren't perfect or the idea isn't fully formed. That act of drawing creates momentum. It makes the invisible visible, and it invites collaboration. It also builds trust, while showing that being the leader doesn't mean you have all the answers. You simply have the courage to start.

Most importantly, this visualization turns abstract strategy into shared ownership. When people can begin to see the vision, they can help shape it.

When they shape it, they believe in it. And when they believe in it, they build it with you.

"*Leadership isn't just about talking—*
*it's about showing. The empty sheet is your stage.*"

In the end, the empty sheet is a stage. It is where leaders turn silence into sense of clarity, and clarity into shared ownership. A single sketch can elevate a meeting, inspire a team, shape a project, and even influence a culture. It turns ideas into something visible and co-owned. Leadership is not just about words; Leadership is about showing. And when you invite others to co-create on that canvas, you build strategies and belief. That is the true power of the white space. Possibility into progress; progress into impact. From white space to impact.

## Key Takeaways

- Clarity around a project rarely appears fully formed. It starts rough. It's a sketch, a line, a shape, an idea pulled out of the fog and put where people can see it. Leaders who draw to think don't wait for perfection; they create momentum by going first. A simple visual often unlocks what paragraphs of text can't. It gives teams something to react to, refine, and build together.

- Tools don't matter as much as engagement. Whiteboards, sticky notes, digital canvases—anything that gets people leaning in, adding ideas, and shaping the picture together becomes a catalyst for alignment. When leaders invite participation, ownership grows. When the work becomes visible, strategy becomes real. And when teams co-create, connection deepens.

- The act of drawing is part of the journey. It slows the mind just enough to see patterns, expose assumptions, and turn abstract thinking into shared understanding.

## Questions to Consider

- What is one idea, challenge, or strategy you could sketch—even roughly—to help your team see what you're thinking?

- How can you make your next planning session more visual so people can react, refine, and co-create?

- Where could a simple diagram or flow help reduce confusion or accelerate alignment?

# Chapter 9:
# The Sound of Global Leadership

For many, success is measured by long hours, but I've learned that you can find success in the right rhythm. And once that rhythm takes hold, the harmony of achievement becomes undeniable.

I've learned that leadership has a sound. Sometimes it's the hum of a boardroom projector, the buzz of voices debating strategy, or the quiet click of keyboards across time zones. But the most powerful sound is rhythm—the cadence of people connecting, aligning, and moving together. In 2004, I hosted 130 global IT leaders under one roof, and I realized I needed more than strategy to build the global team I envisioned. We needed harmony, and harmony, I discovered, can begin with a single note.

For two days, we gathered to discuss regional developments, explore transformational projects, and align on future technology deployments. It was a masterclass in strategic collaboration, but the real magic happened after hours.

*"Music, laughter, and shared rhythm can do*
*what no org chart ever could: build a winning team."*

One of my key goals was to strengthen relationships among leaders and project managers. Because success isn't just about systems; it's about people. It's about achieving goals with ONE global team, working together. And then, the fastest way to build trust isn't through a spreadsheet, but through a shared laugh, a song, or a spontaneous jam session.

So, here was my idea: What if we formed a company band?

One evening, the group meeting transformed into a celebration. In preparation, we reached out to a few colleagues we knew moonlighted as musicians. One team member arrived in full Scottish regalia, bagpipe in hand. He opened the night with a stirring rendition of "Amazing Grace," walking into the room as the notes filled the air. It was a breathtaking sight and an unforgettable start. A stage was set, iconic songs from around the world were chosen, and a few brave souls stepped up to form the first-ever global IT band. Rhythm instruments were placed at every table so everyone could join in.

As the band played, the room came alive. People clapped, sang, and banged. Titles, regions, and roles no longer mattered. In no time, the entire room was in sync, celebrating not just the work, but the joy of working together.

## Culture in Rhythm

The energy in the room was electric. Barriers melted. People who had only exchanged emails were suddenly harmonizing. The rhythm became a metaphor for collaboration, with each person playing their part, listening to others, and contributing to something bigger than themselves. It was a party disguised as a leadership lesson.

That night reinforced a core truth I've always believed: Culture is built in moments. In hallway conversations, shared meals, and yes, even in impromptu concerts. When people feel connected, they work better. They solve faster. They lead with more heart.

*"You can have the best strategy in the world,*
*but if your team isn't having fun together,*
*you're missing the magic."*

# A Moment in the Snow

As our evening of music came to a close, we stepped outside into the night and were greeted by falling snow. A soft white cover blanketed the road. For many, it was a quiet end to a joyful day. But for our Brazilian colleagues, it was the first snowfall they had ever experienced.

Their faces lit with wonder and joy. Laughter echoed in the cold air, and in that moment, I saw what true connection looks like. Shared awe, spontaneous celebration, and the kind of memory that lasts a lifetime.

In the end, leadership is less about milestones and more about moments that echo long after the meeting ends. That night of music and laughter proved that rhythm builds trust faster than any org chart, and joy strengthens collaboration more than any KPI. And when we walked out to that snow, I saw what global leadership truly means. It's connection that transcends borders, titles, and time zones. The lesson is simple but enduring: Strategy sets the stage, but rhythm makes the performance unforgettable.

## Key Takeaways

- Leadership has a rhythm . . . a pulse you feel long before you see it. In global teams, that rhythm is shaped by goals and deliverables, but more importantly, it's the moments in between. Trust grows in shared experiences: the hallway conversations, the late-night meals, the unexpected laughter, the music that fills a room after a long day. Culture doesn't live in presentations; it lives in these moments.

- Joy is strategic. A team that laughs together works differently. That team has more openness, resilience, and willingness to go the extra mile. When leaders celebrate people, not just performance, they create an environment where collaboration becomes natural and connection becomes strength.

- Sometimes leadership means throwing away the script. Do something unexpected. Create a moment that reminds people they're more than their roles. These shared memories become anchors. They remind teams that leadership isn't only about long hours or tough decisions. It's about heart. It's about rhythm. It's about creating experiences that stay with people long after the work is done.

- Global leadership sounds like many things—laughter, conversation, music, footsteps in a hallway—but at its core, it sounds like connection. When leaders tune into that rhythm, teams don't just follow. They flourish.

## Questions to Consider

- What is one small moment you can create this week to strengthen connection within your team?

- How can you intentionally bring more joy or lightness into your leadership rhythm—especially during high-pressure periods?

- What cultural moments—meals, music, traditions—could you highlight or celebrate to deepen global connection?

- How can you make space for the human side of leadership, not just the operational side, in your next team interaction?

# Chapter 10:
# What Culture Taught Me About Leadership

I used to believe adaptation was about systems, new strategies, processes, and tools. But over time, conversations in different places and moments shifted that view. Around 2007, I was pulled aside and asked, quietly but firmly, if we could slow the pace of change. It wasn't resistance; people were simply struggling to lead their teams with confidence. Moments like this reminded me that adaptation isn't optional, but it must be human.

Not everything is about speed. Empathy needs to also be in the mix. When your work is global, adaptation takes on another dimension: cultural awareness or a deep understanding about global culture differences. Leadership across borders starts not with strategy, but with understanding.

The team member of my management team who asked if we could slow down the pace of changes said the pace was wearing on him, and making it harder to lead his team. We sat down, and as we talked, the message that rose is one I believe deeply. I'll always support my team, but adaptation isn't optional. It's not a phase. It's the world we live in. And it's coming at us faster than we ask for.

Adaptation has many faces in leadership. Don't fight it. Befriend it. Use it. Let it sharpen your instincts and expand your reach. Adaptation is global. Your work is global. Your team is global. That's where another layer of leadership comes in: cultural adaptation in global teamwork.

Take a step back and look at your projects. Think about how they were executed. When I reflect on the diverse structures and performances of my teams, three things always rise to the top: understanding, relationships, and team dynamics.

Do we truly understand each other? Are we building strong relationships across borders? Does the team feel aligned, even when spread across time zones and cultures? These aren't easy questions. but they're essential.

Let's explore what happens when cultural adaptation becomes a leadership priority. The charts below show how global team performance transforms when culture is embraced.

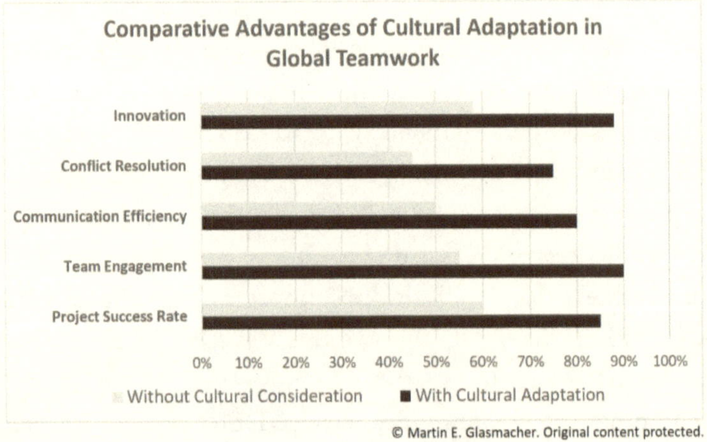




The chart compares key performance metrics between teams that embrace cultural differences and those that don't. Teams that adapt culturally simply perform better. When people understand each other's norms and expectations, projects succeed more often, communication gets smoother, conflicts resolve faster, and innovation rises. Cultural awareness is a performance multiplier.

## 'hat the Numbers Reflect

| Metric | Why Cultural Adaptation Boosts It |
|---|---|
| **Project Success Rate** | Teams that understand cultural norms avoid missteps and align faster on goals. |
| **Team Engagement** | Respecting cultural differences builds trust, inclusion, and motivation. |
| **Communication Efficiency** | Fewer misunderstandings, clearer expectations, and smoother feedback loops. |
| **Conflict Resolution** | Cultural awareness helps leaders navigate tension with empathy and context. |
| **Innovation** | Diverse perspectives flourish when people feel heard and respected. |

*teams begin their cultural learning journey, progress is gradual. But once ndational understanding is in place (like shared norms, trust, and communication 'es), efficiency accelerates dramatically.*

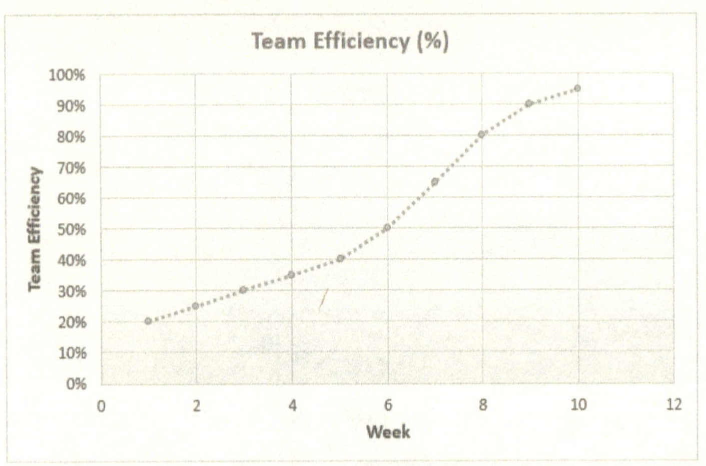



*The Cultural Curve: investing in understanding*

## What This Chart Reveals

- Weeks 1–5: Teams are absorbing cultural nuances, adjusting behaviors, and building trust. Efficiency rises slowly.

- Weeks 6–10: With shared understanding and aligned expectations, collaboration becomes seamless. Efficiency spikes.

- Peak Performance: By week 10, teams operate at 95% efficiency—working across borders as if in the same room.

## Translating Cultural Awareness into Real Life

So how do we bring all this into the real world? How do we move from insight to impact?

Throughout this book, I've shared challenges in inter-cultural and cross-cultural management. These are the moments where misalignment threatened progress, and I've demonstrated how we turned those difficul moments into growth. People want to learn. They want to be part of the journey. As leaders, it's our job to show them why cultural awareness isn't just helpful; it's instrumental.

I remember a situation where team members in the U.S. came to me, frustrated and confused. They'd received emails from colleagues in another part of the world and didn't know how to interpret them. The tone felt off. The style was too direct. The response times were unexpected. And the amount of research and detail without any prior discussion made them feel excluded . . . like they weren't part of the process.

This wasn't a language issue. It was a culture issue.

I explained the communication norms of the other region, helped translate not just the words but the intent, and opened a dialogue between the teams. That moment became a watershed moment for understanding and for trust. What follows are intentional moves we made, each one of which became part of a larger pattern.

- We hosted inter- and cross-cultural management workshops, bringing folks together in person to learn, laugh, and lead.

- We rotated project meetings across global locations, giving each region a chance to host, lead, and shape the agenda.

- We offered team members the chance to work for a few months in a different part of the world. This gave an opportunity to immerse themselves in new cultures, perspectives, and ways of working.

- We assigned leadership roles across cultural zones, ensuring that influence and ownership weren't centralized, but shared.

- And finally: Don't forget the band we formed (see page 52)! It brought people together through rhythm, joy, and shared creativity.

These are strategic actions, but they're also human ones. They build empathy, expand perspective, and unlock performance. If you want maximum results in a multicultural environment, don't just manage culture. Lead through it.

In the end, culture isn't a side note, it's the operating system of global leadership. Charts and metrics prove the impact, but the real lesson lives in the small moments: the misunderstood email, the workshop laughter, the shared rhythm of a band. Those are the places where trust is built and performance unlocked. Leading across borders means more than managing differences. Global leadership means embracing them, translating them, and turning them into strength. When leaders choose to lead through culture, they don't just deliver results; they build bridges, expand horizons, and create teams that move as one . . . even when spread across the world.

## Key Takeaways

- Global leadership starts with understanding before the strategy. Throughout this chapter, one lesson rises above the rest: Adaptation isn't optional, but it must be human. The pace of change may be fast, but people still need clarity, empathy, and the confidence to lead their own teams through uncertainty.

- Working across borders taught me that cultural intelligence isn't something you begin with. It grows through conversations, missteps, shared moments, and the willingness to slow down long enough to truly understand how others think, communicate, and collaborate. When leaders make cultural awareness a priority, performance shifts. Trust deepens. Misunderstandings shrink. Teams move faster because they feel seen.

- The charts in this chapter make the impact visible: higher engagement, clearer communication, stronger innovation. But the real transformation happens in the small moments. The misunderstood email, the workshop laughter, the shared rhythm of a band. These moments remind us that culture isn't a side note. It's the operating system of global leadership.

- When leaders choose to lead through culture, they don't just deliver results. They build bridges, expand horizons, and create teams that move as one, even when spread across the world.

## Questions to Consider

- Where in your team could cultural awareness unlock new levels of trust or performance?

- What is one cultural assumption you can challenge, or one curiosity you can explore, to strengthen a global relationship?

- How can you make communication more inclusive across time zones, styles, and expectations?

- Which recent misunderstanding or friction point could become a learning moment rather than a setback?

# Chapter 11:
# Beyond Networking: Shaping the Future Through Thought Leadership

When I first stepped into SIM, the Society for Information Management in 2008, I thought I was joining a network. What I discovered was something far more powerful: a community. It wasn't about exchanging business cards or attending events. It was about shaping the future of technology leadership *together*. I remember feeling both humbled and energized. Surrounded by some of the most respected IT leaders in the industry, I asked myself: What can I contribute here? The answer became clear. I would give vision, mentorship, and a commitment to turn ideas into impact.

## Where Ideas Meet Execution

In the world of technology leadership, few organizations enjoy the legacy and influence of SIM. Since 1968, SIM has been a nexus for the most respected IT leaders in the industry. When I joined its ranks and later served as co-chair of the program office at SIM Research Triangle Park, NC, I brought credentials and vision.

My involvement with SIM was about helping to shape the future of IT leadership; mentoring emerging talent; and driving conversations around megatrends, digital transformation, and enterprise resilience. And I wasn't alone. We built a community of leaders who challenged each other to think bigger and act smarter.

*"SIM is a space for purposeful leadership—where experience is
shared, ideas are tested, and transformation begins."*

## urating the Future

As co-chair of the program office, I helped design and deliver programs
at explored the tech trends reshaping business and society. From
bersecurity to AI, cloud strategy to digital ethics, we curated conversations
at mattered. Our sessions were grounded in real-world impact and drawn
om my own experiences.

At SIM we didn't just talk about leadership. We practiced it. We created
ace for honest dialogue, cross-industry learning, and actionable insights.
or me, leadership has never been static. It's a discipline, a mindset, and a
ared responsibility.

## Voice in the Boardroom

I've had the privilege of guiding boards, executive teams, and strategic
mmittees through digital strategy and transformation. My greatest
ntribution was the ability to turn complexity into clarity. I helped leaders
e the path forward, align around bold decisions, and move with confidence.

Whether guiding merger and acquisitions (M&A) decisions, shaping
bersecurity frameworks, or mentoring CIOs, I operated with clearness,
surance, and collaborative rigor. Thoughtful leadership is about enabling
hers to translate ideas into action that drives meaningful results.

## Robots, Youth, and the Future of Innovation

As a board member of the Society for Information Management, I had a front-row seat to the brilliance of the next generation. One of our core missions was to support schools and students with a passion for technology. I'll never forget the day I sat in on a funding hearing where kids pitched their own tech projects.

These kids didn't just talk! They exhibited the robots they built from scratch—machines that moved, sensed, and responded with precision and purpose. Each team was vying for a spot in major league competitions, hoping to bring home a title for their school. Their ingenuity was electric and their confidence contagious. For a moment, I was that wide-eyed kid again, fascinated by the magic of machines.

## Robots: the Game Changer

Have you ever watched a robot in action and felt that spark of wonder? Robotics is cool, but more than that, it's transformative. From manufacturing to medicine and logistics to learning, robots are reshaping industries and redefining possibility. It all starts with young minds, bold ideas, and the courage to build something that moves.

*"Leadership is a practice. You don't inherit it.*
*You earn it, refine it, and share it."*

Ultimately, thought leadership is measured not by titles or panels but by the impact you leave on people and the future they create. SIM taught me that leadership grows stronger when shared and that ideas gain power when vested in community. The next generation is already building the future we imagine. Robots may move precisely, but it is people who move with intent. When leaders choose to amplify others, they shape conversations and possibilities. That is the true power of thought leadership: turning connection into clarity, and clarity into change.

## Key Takeaways

- Thought leadership is a responsibility. It's earned through being clear and consistent. It's also earned through the courage of bringing people together around ideas that matter. Throughout my work with SIM, the TASK series, and the broader technology community, one truth became clear: Leadership expands when you step into spaces where people gather to learn, question, and grow.

- Community amplifies leadership. Great ideas rarely take off in isolation; they need curious, committed, and collaborative people to bring them to life. Whether co-chairing programs at SIM, curating megatrend sessions on AI and cybersecurity, or advising boards on strategy and resilience, the work was never about standing at the front of the room. It was about creating rooms where honest dialogue could happen.

- Thought leadership is earned through practice. It comes from showing up, sharing what you know, and translating complexity into something people can actually use. In a world overflowing with noise, leaders who can make strategy accessible and  can turn megatrends into meaningful action become trusted voices. They help others see what's coming and prepare for what's next.

- And at its core, thought leadership is service. It's about elevating others, strengthening the community, and shaping conversations that move industries forward. When leaders curate discussions that matter, they don't just inform; they inspire. They create momentum. They build bridges across teams, companies, and regions. And they remind us that leadership lives in the impact we make on the people around us.

- Leading through community is leading from a center of connection, not hierarchy. When leaders share openly, listen deeply, and create space for others to grow, they don't just influence the conversation. They shape the future.

## Questions to Consider

- How can you create more space for honest dialogue within your team or professional network?

- What community or professional group could benefit from your experience, and what steps can you take to engage more intentionally?

- How can you use your influence to elevate voices around you, not just your own?

# Chapter 12:
# Coaching and Legacy

I used to believe my greatest achievements would be measured in systems delivered or strategies executed. Over time, I realized the real measure of leadership is not what you build, but *who* you build. Titles fade and projects end, but the leaders you grow carry your impact forward. That's why coaching became my vocation. Every conversation, every workshop, every challenge was a chance to plant seeds of leadership that would outlast my own tenure.

*"You don't grow leaders by giving them answers.*
*You grow them by giving them frameworks*
*and the space to act."*

## Growing Leaders

At Voith, we designed and delivered the TASK (Teamwork, Work Methods, Synergy, and Communication) leadership series: an immersive program for emerging leaders. TASK was based in strategic thinking, execution under pressure, and accountability.

We built TASK to challenge high-potential talent and equip them with the tools to lead. Participants learned, but more importantly, they practiced. They tackled real business problems, presented to executive teams, and received direct coaching from our coaching team. TASK became a cornerstone of our healthy leadership pipeline, and its alumni stepped into key roles throughout the organization.

## Coaching Across Contexts

The TASK workshop itself was designed in two parts, each a five-day intensive with a four-week break in between. That gap was used to introduce a coaching program focused on remote collaboration, preparing teams to work across locations.

The concept was simple but powerful: Launch a cross-location project during the break, giving participants a real-world challenge in an emerging model of virtual teamwork. We assembled diverse teams from different locations and provided a clear guide on tools and methods to succeed. Shared cloud workspaces, regular video calls, and structured collaboration helped recreate the energy of being in the same room, but without the travel.

*"Leadership sparks ripple. Invest in others.*
*Impact multiplies outward."*

Back in early 2000, this was groundbreaking for the business. It laid the foundation for how we operate today: connected across locations and united in purpose. Sitting in their own offices, team members built a shared digital workspace without distance. We saw clearly that this was the future: a modern, efficient way to collaborate, share ideas, and drive results in real time.

Whether I was guiding young technicians and engineers or seasoned executives, I brought the same precision: focus on outcomes, lead with integrity, and never stop learning.

We kept the core coaching team together for nearly four years, delivering fifteen workshop series across multiple cities in Germany and Austria. More an 250 participants joined our TASK sessions. This wasn't your typical class or business meeting. These were handpicked talents, selected by senior leadership to spark a movement. Our mission was to reshape how we collaborate, solve problems, and lead in a world of remote work. What made it truly powerful was the focus on continuous improvement. New habits were embedded into daily work life.

Each workshop became a catalyst for lasting change. We adapted, iterated, and refined together, and that mindset of evolving with purpose became the basis of how I lead and coach today.

My coaching didn't end at Voith. Throughout my career, I've mentored CIOs, advised boards, and supported startup founders. My approach has always been direct, strategic, and empowering. I offered advice, but more importantly, I helped people build their own playbooks. My workshops were coaching tools to unlock potential and elevate teams.

## Key Takeaways

- Every time you manage or lead people, you're coaching. Whether it is guiding someone through a really tough deadline, helping them communicate with stakeholders, or energizing a disengaged team meeting, these are all moments of coaching.

- Some team members need weekly one-on-ones; others need help, feedback, and engagement. Use open-ended questions. Be a sounding board. Let nature and its seasons set your rhythm: prepare the soil, plant, nurture, harvest, and reflect. It's not about giving directions. It's about empowering others to grow. Leadership is coaching.

- Legacy isn't written in code or contracts. It's written in people. The systems we built may evolve, but the leaders we develop continue to shape organizations, communities, and futures. Coaching is not a side task of leadership. Coaching IS leadership.

- When you give frameworks instead of answers, when you stretch people beyond comfort, and when you invest in their growth, you multiply your impact far beyond your own reach. That is the vocation of leadership.

- Leadership is something you practice and refine through action, reflection, and the courage to grow alongside the people you lead.

- At its core, coaching is simple: Be humble, be kind, and make the complex feel clear. Great leaders don't create dependencies; they create frameworks. They give people tools, not answers. They build confidence, not reliance.

- Growth lives just beyond comfort. Stretching people thoughtfully and intentionally is one of the greatest gifts a leader can offer. And the best coaching travels well. It works across industries, cultures, and titles because it's rooted in humanity, not hierarchy.

## Questions to Consider

- Who is one person you can stretch, support, or coach more intentionally this month?

- Where can you simplify a process, expectation, or idea so others can lead with more clarity?

- What framework or tool could you create that helps your team make decisions without you in the room?

- What leadership legacy are you building today, and who is already carrying part of it forward?

# Chapter 13:
# The Thrill and Joy Factor

I used to think grit alone carried teams forward with long hours, relentless focus, and sheer determination. Over time, I discovered other things that are just as powerful: the thrill of a win, the laughter in a meeting, the smile that breaks tension. These are not distractions. They are accelerators. Promoting fulfillment fuels connection, and connection fuels performance. Whether in sports arenas or boardrooms, the energy of happiness transforms effort into momentum. Leadership is about more than driving results. It's also about creating moments that feel like winning together.

For most people, watching their hometown heroes or favorite athletes win is pure magic. It's a surge of joy. Hearts pounding. Arms raised. Voices lifted in triumph.

*"Motivation soars. Bonds deepen.*
*Memories are made."*

Behind every one of those moments? Countless hours of unseen effort. Early mornings. Late nights. Repetition. Recovery. Strategy sessions. Setbacks. Comebacks. It's vision in action. It's perseverance. It's the fire to keep going when no one's watching.

What drives them? The love of the game. The thrill of mastery. The hunger to win. Recognition. Growth. Flow. Shared goals. Team energy. Step by step, they climb. They are fueled by belief, lifted by support, driven by their mission.

And here's the bottom line: Every win deserves attention, whether it's big or small. It deserves reflection and joy. It deserves celebration.

How do we create moments like that at work? Can you imagine channeling that same energy into your next project or team meeting? How do you create that excitement, unity, and drive?

To move anything forward, you need vision and ideas. But here's the reality: Nothing worthwhile comes easy. It takes time. It takes tenacity. It takes showing up when it's hard, and staying in when it counts. And yet, when you pair determination with joy, when you add a smile to the hustle, you don't just move faster. You move better. You build momentum. You create something magnetic. You make work feel like winning.

Smiling is a mood that acts as an engine of connection. Walk into a room with a genuine smile, and the atmosphere transforms. Tension melts, shoulders drop, and the team exhales. A smile lifts morale, raises energy levels, and helps spark connection. It's contagious and magnetic. It's leadership in motion.

And what follows? More than just bright moments—turning points. Stories of joy, connection, and shared humanity that don't just light the way forward but reshape it. They open new ground. They make space for what comes next.

## Milan, Italy: Joy in the Details

An unforgettable moment from my entrepreneurial journey unfolded in Milan. I traveled with my co-founder and close friend Guenter and his wife, Ruth, for an investor meeting about a new real estate development. We had just completed a condominium complex *"Sturmsberg"* in our hometown that ended up being a two-year journey from blueprint to final touch.

We felt the magnitude of every truckload of concrete we poured, every floor that rose, and every meeting about progress, challenges, timelines, and costs. The movement. The momentum. The joy. It wasn't just a project. It was a shared win, and what a time it was.

In Milan, we were chasing the next opportunity.

An Italian businessman had reached out, inviting us to explore a new venture. We came prepared, and the meeting was electric, with high energy, high motivation, and high stakes. We soaked in the cultural distinction, the rhythm of cross-border business, the power of communication beyond language.

*"Joy sparked connection.*
*Effort became ease. Bonds endure."*

Afterward, Guenter, Ruth, and I sat outside at a sun-drenched Milanese café, replaying all the details. We talked over every word, gesture, and insight. There was joy reviewing the details. It reminded us that the best moments in business aren't just about deals. They're about connection, curiosity, and the thrill of what's next. And yes, we got the contract.

## York, PA: Reflection and Laughter as Leadership

One evening in York, Pennsylvania, I sat with my senior management team for hours without our spreadsheets and strategy decks. Just stories.

We came together as people, undefined by rank or responsibilities. We shared memories from the trenches of long hours, tight deadlines, big wins, and quiet victories. We laughed about the chaos, the close calls, the creative pivots. We reached back into our youth, swapping tales that made us smile and connect. Laughter echoed around the room. So did trust.

That night, we built a foundation forged in laughter, respect, and shared experience. This carried us through future challenges, changes, and growth. We still talk about this time, because we built it, together.

## Cincinnati, OH: The Power of a Selfie

At a big group meeting in Cincinnati, I took a risk. The night before, I'd snapped a selfie with teammates and friends from around the Americas. It was a joyful moment, and my peers asked me to add the selfie to my slides, and I promised them I'd share it during my presentation the next day. Not exactly standard conference material, but I went for it.

The next morning, we kicked off the meeting as usual. I delivered my speech, hit the key points, and walked everyone through the slides. And then, just before closing, there it was: the selfie. Full screen. Beaming out to 200 people.

The reaction was instant. Laughter filled the room, and the energy shifted. I echoed our CEO's opening line: "Borderless leadership, timeless impact."

And suddenly, the message landed. Humor made it human. Connection made it real. Happiness holds power, joy builds trust, and promises stays kept.

## Raleigh, NC: Leadership Is About Giving

Thanksgiving reminds me that leadership is about vision and presence. It's about showing up, even when no one's watching, and giving without expecting anything in return.

For several years, I'd head to the supermarket and fill my cart with pumpkin pies. They weren't for a dinner party or a meeting; they were just for giving away. I'd spend the day driving through town, stopping by friends' homes, handing out pies, sharing a quick laugh or a quiet moment, and then moving on.

Downtown, I'd visit homeless shelters and drop off pies for folks who needed a little comfort. I'd greet people hanging out on the street playing music, sitting, or watching the day unfold. I'd stop, say hello, hand them a pie, and wish them a Happy Thanksgiving. No speeches. Just a pie.

Those moments taught me that leadership lives in the small gestures. A pie. A smile. A few minutes of genuine connection. That's what builds trust.

Moments like handing out pie also reminded me that leadership is about giving, especially when it matters most.

In business, we chase goals and deadlines, but real impact comes when we pause to support our people. I've had team members facing deep personal struggles. In those moments, the right move wasn't strategic—it was human. Putting people first, being present, and giving without expecting. That's leadership. That's legacy.

Joy is not the opposite of discipline. It's the multiplier of it. It doesn't make a team lose focus, but instead helps the team reset. Strategy sets the plan, and persistence delivers the effort, but the feeling of fulfillment makes it sustainable. A quick moment of humor lowers tension so people can return to the work sharper. A smile can shift a room, laughter can build trust, and small acts of kindness can leave legacies greater than any milestone.

Leadership lives in those moments when determination meets delight, when giving meets gratitude, and when work feels like winning. That is the thrill and joy factor: leading with light, so others can see the path forward more clearly, and walk it with you. When joy is paired with a sense of fulfillment and truly knowing the work matters, teams stay disciplined and energized at the same time.

## Key Takeaways

- Joy is a driver. Happy teams think differently. They're more creative, more resilient, and more willing to take the kinds of risks that move organizations forward. Motivation fuels momentum, especially in moments of uncertainty, and leaders set the emotional tone that makes that possible.

- When leaders show up with light, be it a smile, a sense of possibility, or a moment of levity, they create psychological safety. People feel free to contribute, to challenge, and to try. Joy becomes a signal that it's safe to show up fully. It's safe to care.

- Leading with light doesn't mean ignoring pressure. It means balancing it. It means reminding teams that progress can be energizing, not exhausting. Making sure people know that work can be meaningful and joyful at the same time. When leaders model that balance, teams thrive.

## Questions to Consider

- What is one small moment of joy you can intentionally create for your team this week?

- Where could joy or levity help reduce tension and unlock creativity during a challenging project?

- What motivates your team right now, and how can you amplify it to build momentum?

- How can you make joy a consistent leadership practice, instead of an occasional surprise?

# Chapter 14:
# Reflections & Future Vision

Looking back at my unconventional path, a few principles stand out. Leadership is not about titles or milestones. It's about providing a crystal-clear vision for your team and your company.

Also, I've learned that strategy only matters if it becomes stewardship. Systems fade, products evolve, but the leaders you elevate endure. My journey has been about turning vision into action and about ensuring that action builds something lasting.

Throughout my career, strategic clarity has been my motivating principle. I've led by motivating people who felt like valued members of the equation. They knew complex challenges couldn't be solved without them.

I built systems and defined processes that scaled and coached leaders who now shape their own organizations. I've founded companies, created products, and invested with purpose. But beyond all this, my legacy is built on something deeper. I turned vision into action.

> *"Success isn't a destination. It's the discipline*
> *of showing up every single day,*
> *solving problems, and empowering others."*

Today, I'm exploring new technologies, taking AI classes, continuing to mentor the next generation of leaders, and staying deeply engaged in the conversations that matter. As an investor, I draw on years of experience with tech companies, strong leadership teams, and breakthrough products to guide my decisions. I'm reconnecting with the entrepreneurial spirit that sparked my journey years ago by maintaining a blog and shaping the next chapter of my story. For me, it feels like going back to the future.

I'm also documenting my legacy for my family, good friends, and future collaborators. This book is part of that legacy: a blueprint for strategic leadership, a reflection on what works, and a challenge to think bigger.

*"The future belongs to those who build it.*
*And building starts with clarity,*
*courage, and commitment."*

## A Message to Future Leaders

To those stepping into leadership roles, I offer this:

- Lead with purpose, not ego.

- Think in scenarios; act with discipline.

- Invest in your own growth and in others'.

- Build systems and processes that empower people.

Leadership isn't about control. It is about stewardship. It's about leaving things better than you found them. And it's about knowing that your impact is measured not just in results, but in the people you elevate along the way.

Ultimately, legacy is not measured in what you leave behind, but instead measured in the people who carry your lessons forward. Strategic clarity is the compass, courage is the fuel, and commitment is the rhythm that sustains the journey. The future belongs to those who build it, and building begins with light, with clarity, and with bravery. My hope is that these reflections spark action, this unconventional perspective fosters stewardship, and the impact endures in others.

## Key Takeaways

- Clarity, courage, commitment, and legacy are the anchors of leadership, especially when the path ahead is complex. Strategic clarity becomes the compass. It helps you see what matters, cut through noise, and make the hard calls with conviction. Leadership, at its best, is stewardship. It's the choice to invest in people, not just outcomes, and to build something that lasts long after the work is done.

- Curiosity keeps leaders moving forward. It fuels reinvention, opens new doors, and shapes the legacy you leave behind. And sharing your story—the lessons, the missteps, the moments that shaped you— becomes part of that legacy. Your experience can light the path for others, giving them the courage to lead in their own way.

- In the end, legacy lives in people. In those you've elevated, empowered, and encouraged. In the leaders who step forward stronger because you once stood beside them. The future of leadership is built in community, carried forward by the people you've lifted along the way.

## Questions to Consider

- What clarity do you need right now to navigate the next phase of your leadership journey?

- How can you recommit to the people and priorities that matter most?

- What part of your story could help someone else lead with more confidence or perspective?

- Who are you lifting today, and how will they carry your legacy forward?

# Chapter 15:
# Leadership at a Glance

This final chapter is not another story, but a compass. It's designed for the leader who needs clarity before a meeting, courage before a decision, or connection before a conversation. Here you'll find the essence of this journey distilled into lessons, tables, and questions that turn reflection into action. Because leadership is not about remembering everything. It is about carrying forward what matters most.

Following a path shaped by experiences, insights, and lessons, this chapter condenses the core of *Leading with Purpose* into a concise, practical guide. It's designed for leaders who want to revisit key insights quickly. Whether you are preparing for a team meeting, mentoring a rising executive, or reflecting on your own growth, you will find answers here. By organizing the book's core themes into tables, charts, and questions, this chapter becomes a practical tool for action and alignment.

Here, you'll find the leadership principles that emerged across borders and industries—clarity in crisis, courage in decision-making, and connection across cultures. From tips on remote collaboration to reflections on legacy, each section offers a compressed dose of wisdom. This isn't just a summary—it's a blueprint. A way to carry the heart of this book into your daily leadership practice.

# Leadership at a Glance

## Compressed Wisdom from a Global Journey

### ✳ Leadership Lessons Table

| Chapter | Theme | Key Leadership Lessons |
|---|---|---|
| Startup Energy | Systems Thinking | Start with structure, scale with clarity. Design systems that reflect real values and adapt to complexity. |
| From Prototype to Platform | Innovation | Build trust through iteration. Innovation isn't a one-time spark - it's a rhythm of testing, listening, and refining until trust becomes traction. |
| Coaching & Legacy | Mentorship | Legacy lives in others. True leadership is measured not by what you build, but by who you empower to build after you. |
| From white Space to Impact | Visualization | Use shared visuals early. Diagrams, metaphors, and sketches aren't decoration. |
| Global Perspective | Cultural Agility | Make it visible. Draw it. Invite others to shape it. Leadership across borders requires humility, clarity, and shared language. |
| Reflections & Future Vision | Stewardship | Elevate others. Share your story. Stewardship means designing for continuity - so your impact lives on in people, processes, and purpose. |

### ❓ Leadership Q&A Grid

| Question | Insight |
|---|---|
| How do I lead across cultures? | Learn the rhythms, invest in empathy, and prepare intentionally |
| What builds trust in crisis? | Show up, stay visible, and own the message |
| How do I coach future leaders? | Share frameworks, stretch their thinking, and celebrate their growth |
| What makes strategy stick? | Make it visible. Draw it. Invite others to shape it |
| How do I leave a legacy? | Elevate others. Share your story. Build systems that last |

### 🛠 Tips & Tricks Chart

| Situation | Tip |
|---|---|
| Starting a global project | Host a cultural workshop first |
| Leading a remote team | Embed rhythm and presence |
| Navigating tough decisions | Think in scenarios, act with discipline |
| Building alignment | Use shared visuals early |
| Coaching a new leader | Ask, listen, stretch, repeat |

#### Understanding Culture & Collaboration

- Rotate facilitation roles in global team meetings
- Prepare for small talk in U.S. settings; clarify tone in emails abroad
- Host cultural workshops to strengthen cross-border teamwork

#### Your Leadership Blueprint

**CLARITY + COURAGE + CONNECTION + CULTURE = IMPACT**

# UNCONVENTIONAL
## LEADERSHIP
### Gearbox Strategy

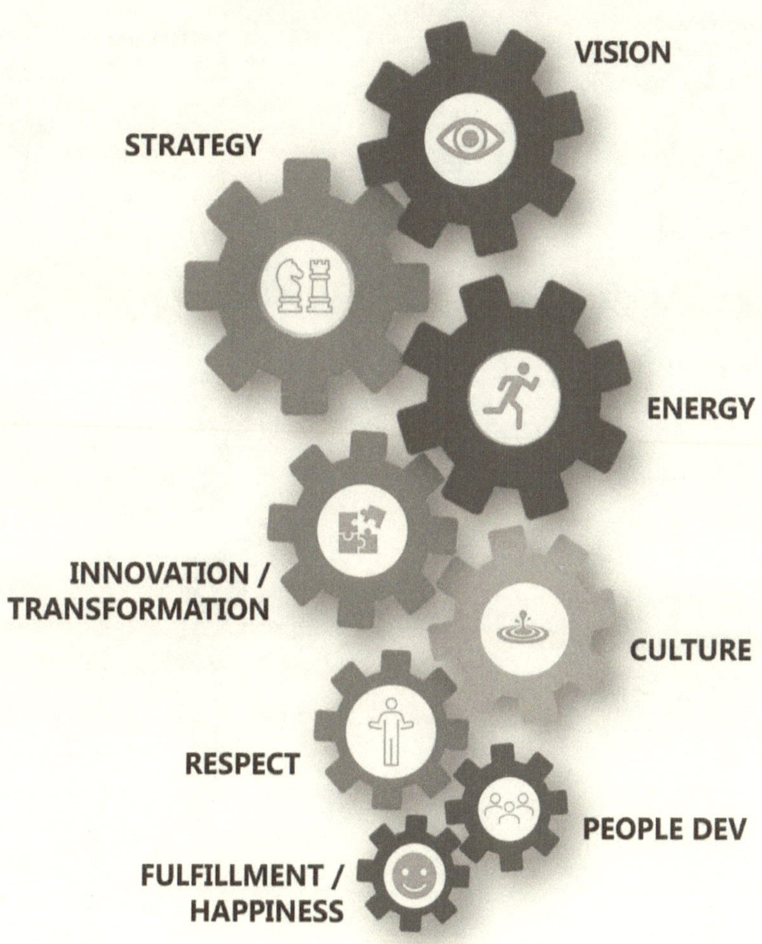


**Industries Served**

Manufacturing | Engineering | Technology | Digital | Field
Services | Energy | Construction | Real Estate | Insurance

# Leading From The Center
## Crisis Management

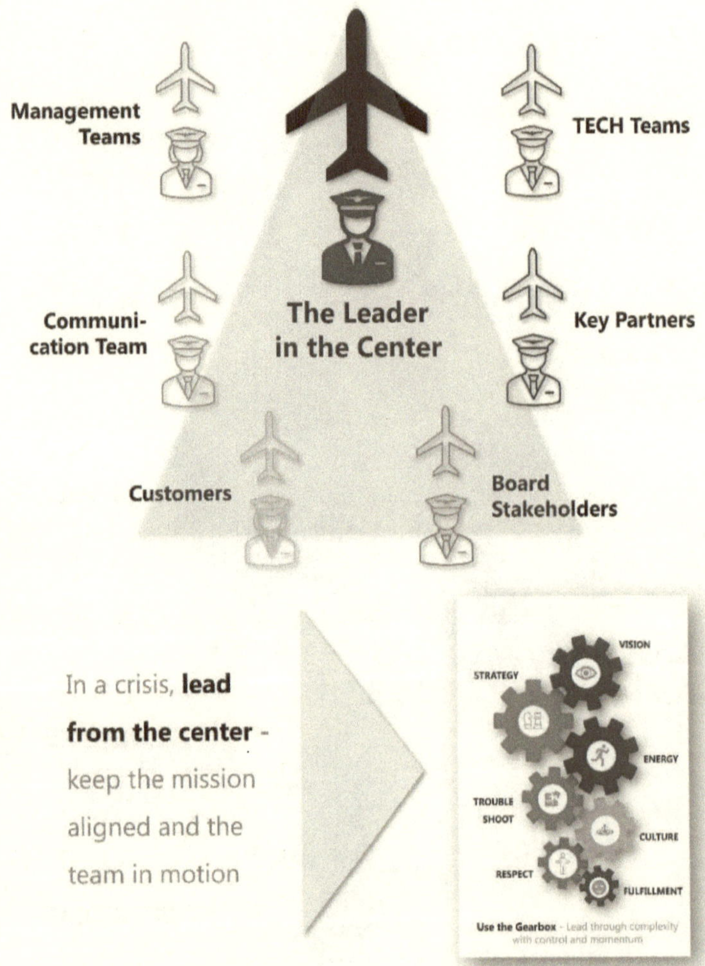

# Leadership Lessons Table

| Chapter | Theme | Key Leadership Lessons |
| --- | --- | --- |
| Tech-Driven, Purpose-Led | Biz Process-Systems Thinking | Start with structure, scale with clarity |
| From Prototype to Platform | Innovation | Build trust through iteration |
| Coaching & Legacy | Mentorship | Empowering others creates ripple effects |
| Global Perspective | Cultural Agility | Translate strategy across borders |
| White Space to Impact | Visualization | Draw to align, lead by sketching |
| Reflections & Future Vision | Stewardship | Legacy lives in others |

# Culture & Collaboration Table

Key Insights for Leading Across Borders

| Topic | Insight | Tip |
| --- | --- | --- |
| German vs. American Communication | Germans tend to be direct and task-focused; Americans often prioritize rapport and optimism. | Prepare for small talk in U.S. meetings; clarify tone in cross-cultural communication. |
| Cultural Fluency | Understanding cultural norms builds trust and prevents misalignment. | Invest in intercultural coaching before major transitions. |
| Global Team Meetings | Cultural expectations shape participation and decision-making. | Rotate facilitation roles and clarify expectations upfront. |
| Email Etiquette | Tone and structure vary widely across cultures. | Use neutral language and avoid idioms; clarify intent when needed. |
| Feedback Styles | Some cultures value direct critique; others prefer indirect suggestions. | Ask how feedback is best received; don't assume. |
| Leadership Presence | Visibility and rhythm matter across time zones. | Schedule regular check-ins and show up consistently. |
| Celebrating Together | Shared experiences build trust and team identity. | Create moments of joy like music, stories, or cultural exchange. |
| Learning Across Cultures | Teams thrive when they understand each other's context. | Host workshops on cultural dynamics and global collaboration. |

| Question | Insight |
| --- | --- |
| How do I lead across cultures? | Learn the rhythms, invest in empathy, and prepare intentionally. |
| What builds trust in crisis? | Show up, stay visible, and own the message. |
| How do I coach future leaders? | Share frameworks, stretch their thinking, and celebrate their growth. |
| What makes strategy stick? | Make it visible. Draw it. Invite others to shape it. |
| How do I leave a legacy? | Elevate others. Share your story. Build systems that last. |

# Tips & Tricks Chart

| Situation | Tip |
| --- | --- |
| Starting a global project | Host a cultural workshop first |
| Leading a remote team | Embed rhythm and presence |
| Navigating tough decisions | Think in scenarios, act with discipline |
| Building alignment | Use shared visuals early |
| Coaching a new leader | Ask, listen, stretch, repeat |

## Your Leadership Blueprint

**CLARITY + COURAGE + CONNECTION + CULTURE = IMPACT**

Clarity sets direction. Courage drives action. Connection builds trust. Culture bridges borders. Together, they create an impact that lasts.

I hope you carry forward more than just stories. I hope you've found real leadership insight, grounded in global experience and tested in real business scenarios.

If my journey has sparked new ways of thinking, leading, and growing then I've done my job. May these reflections help you shape your own rhythm, build your own systems and processes, and lead with clarity wherever your path takes you next.

This book is not meant to be shelved. I want you to live it. My hope is that these lessons serve as a rhythm you can return to, a blueprint you can adapt, and a reminder that leadership is not about control, but about impact. Carry these principles into your own journey, and let them light the path for others. Because leadership isn't just about milestones. It's about moments. Those moments, lived with clarity and courage, become the legacy we leave behind.

# Acknowledgments

I owe special thanks to my friend Luis Bermudez, whose thoughtful critique, structural guidance, and steady presence helped this manuscript find its true shape. He invested not just time, but heart and honesty into the process. His contribution sits between the lines of these pages, and I'm deeply grateful for the generosity and friendship behind it.

To the executives and board members who trusted me with bold decisions and complex transformations: thank you for your confidence, your candor, and your partnership. You challenged me to think strategically and act decisively, and I'm grateful for every moment of shared leadership.

To my family, especially my wife, Uschi, and daughter, Lea: thank you for your unwavering support, your love, and your belief in me through every chapter of this journey. You are my foundation, my inspiration, and my greatest joy.

To my close friends and colleagues: thank you for the laughter, the late-night brainstorms, the honest feedback, and the unforgettable memories. You've made the work meaningful and the journey worthwhile.

This book is for all of you and for everyone who believes that with hard work, kindness, and a clear vision, we can build something truly extraordinary.

# About the Author

Martin E. Glasmacher's leadership story is one of global scale and human depth. From his early technology roots in Germany to transformative executive roles in the United States, he has navigated industries, cultures, and decades of change. Building lasting high-performing teams and scaling enterprise systems and processes with precision and a people-first mentality is his forte. Known for blending strategic insight with entrepreneurial grit, Martin now turns his focus to coaching and writing, sharing hard-earned lessons and timeless values.

His mission: to empower the next generation to lead with vision, clarity, and kindness. This book is both a reflection and a roadmap. This is an invitation to chart your own path with courage and purpose.

**Online Companion to Unconventional Leadership**

## EMGEX

Leadership. Powered by AI.

www.emgex.ai

www.ingramcontent.com/pod-product-compliance
Lightning Source LLC
Chambersburg PA
CBHW061437160726
47995CB00003B/936